Oration by Frederick Douglass, Delivered on the Occasion of the Unveiling of the Freedmen's Monument in Memory of Abraham Lincoln, in Lincoln Park, Washington, D.C., April 14th, 1876. With an Appendix

ORATION.

Friends and Fellow-Citizens:

I warmly congratulate you upon the highly interesting object which has caused you to assemble in such numbers and spirit as you have to-day. This occasion is in some respects remarkable. Wise and thoughtful men of our race, who shall come after us, and study the lesson of our history in the United States; who shall survey the long and dreary spaces over which we have travelled; who shall count the links in the great chain of events by which we have reached our present position, will make a note of this occasion; they will think of it and speak of it with a sense of manly pride and complacency.

I congratulate you, also, upon the very favorable circumstances in which we meet to-day. They are high, inspiring, and uncommon. They lend grace, glory, and significance to the object for which we have met. Nowhere else in this great country, with its uncounted towns and cities, unlimited wealth, and immeasurable territory extending from sea to sea, could conditions be found more favorable to the success of this occasion than here.

We stand to-day at the national centre to perform something like a national act—an act which is to go into history; and we are here where every pulsation of the national heart can be heard, felt, and reciprocated. A thousand wires, fed with thought and winged with lightning, put us in instantaneous communication with the loyal and true men all over this country.

Few facts could better illustrate the vast and wonderful

change which has taken place in our condition as a people than the fact of our assembling here for the purpose we have to day. Harmless, beautiful, proper, and praiseworthy as this demonstration is, I cannot forget that no such demonstration would have been tolerated here twenty years ago. The spirit of slavery and barbarism, which still lingers to blight and destroy in some dark and distant parts of our country, would have made our assembling here the signal and excuse for opening upon us all the flood-gates of wrath and violence. That we are here in peace to-day is a compliment and a credit to American civilization, and a prophecy of still greater national enlightenment and progress in the future. I refer to the past not in malice, for this is no day for malice; but simply to place more distinctly in front the gratifying and glorious change which has come both to our white fellow citizens and ourselves, and to congratulate all upon the contrast between now and then; the new dispensation of freedom with its thousand blessings to both races, and the old dispensation of slavery with its ten thousand evils to both races — white and black. In view, then, of the past, the present, and the future, with the long and dark history of our bondage behind us, and with liberty, progress, and enlightenment before us, I again congratulate you upon this auspicious day and hour.

Friends and fellow citizens, the story of our presence here is soon and easily told. We are here in the District of Columbia, here in the city of Washington, the most luminous point of American territory; a city recently transformed and made beautiful in its body and in its spirit; we are here in the place where the ablest and best men of the country are sent to devise the policy, enact the laws, and shape the destiny of the Republic; we are here, with the stately pillars and majestic dome of the Capitol of the nation looking down upon us; we are here, with the broad earth freshly adorned with the foliage and flowers of spring for our church, and all races, colors, and conditions of men for our congregation—in a word, we are here to express, as best we may, by appropriate forms and ceremonies, our grateful sense of the vast, high, and pre-eminent services rendered to ourselves, to our race, to our country, and to the whole world by Abraham Lincoln.

The sentiment that brings us here to-day is one of the noblest that can stir and thrill the human heart. It has crowned and made glorious the high places of all civilized nations with the grandest and most enduring works of art, designed to illustrate the characters and perpetuate the memories of great public men. It is the sentiment which from year to year adorns with fragrant and beautiful flowers the graves of our loyal, brave, and patriotic soldiers who fell in defence of the Union and liberty. It is the sentiment of gratitude and appreciation, which often in presence of many who hear me, has filled yonder heights of Arlington with the eloquence of eulogy and the sublime enthusiasm of poetry and song; a sentiment which can never die while the Republic lives.

For the first time in the history of our people, and in the history of the whole American people, we join in this high worship, and march conspicuously in the line of this time-honored custom. First things are always interesting, and this is one of our first things. It is the first time that in this form and manner, we have sought to do honor to an American great man, however deserving and illustrious. I commend the fact to notice; let it be told in every part of the Republic; let men of all parties and opinions hear it; to those who despise us, not less than those who respect us, know that now and here in the spirit of liberty, loyalty, and gratitude, let it be known everywhere, and by everybody who takes an interest in human progress and in the amelioration of the condition of mankind, that, in the presence and with the approval of the members of the American House of Representatives, reflecting

4

the general sentiment of the country; that in the presence of
that august body, the American Senate, representing the high
est intelligence and the calmest judgment of the country; in
presence of the Supreme Court and Chief Justice of the United
States, to whose decisions we all patriotically bow; in the presence and under the steady eye of the honored and trusted
President of the United States, with the members of his wise
and patriotic Cabinet, we, the colored people, newly emancipated and rejoicing in our blood-bought freedom, near the
close of the first century in the life of this Republic, have
now and here unveiled, set apart, and dedicated a monument
of enduring granite and bronze, in every line, feature, and
figure of which the men of this generation may read, and
those of after-coming generations may read, something of
the exalted character and great works of Abraham Lincoln, the
first martyr President of the United States.

Fellow-citizens, in what we have said and done to day, and
in what we may say and do hereafter, we disclaim everything
like arrogance and assumption. We claim for ourselves no
superior devotion to the character, history, and memory of the
illustrious name whose monument we have here dedicated
to day. We fully comprehend the relation of Abraham Lincoln
both to ourselves and to the white people of the United States.
Truth is proper and beautiful at all times and in all places,
and it is never more proper and beautiful in any case than
when speaking of a great public man whose example is likely
to be commended for honor and imitation long after his de-
parture to the solemn shades, the silent continents of eternity.
It must be admitted, truth compels me to admit, even here in
the presence of the monument we have erected to his memory,
Abraham Lincoln was not, in the fullest sense of the word,
either our man or our model. In his interests, in his associa-
tions, in his habits of thought, and in his prejudices, he was
a white man.

He was pre-eminently the white man's President, entirely devoted to the welfare of white men. He was ready and willing at any time during the first years of his administration to deny, postpone, and sacrifice the rights of humanity in the colored people to promote the welfare of the white people of this country. In all his education and feeling he was an American of the Americans. He came into the Presidential chair upon one principle alone, namely, opposition to the extension of slavery. His arguments in furtherance of this policy had their motive and mainspring in his patriotic devotion to the interests of his own race. To protect, defend, and perpetuate slavery in the States where it existed Abraham Lincoln was not less ready than any other President to draw the sword of the nation. He was ready to execute all the supposed constitutional guarantees of the United States Constitution in favor of the slave system anywhere inside the slave States. He was willing to pursue, recapture, and send back the fugitive slave to his master, and to suppress a slave rising for liberty, though his guilty master were already in arms against the Government. The race to which we belong were not the special objects of his consideration. Knowing this, I concede to you, my white fellow-citizens, a pre-eminence in this worship at once full and supreme. First, midst, and last, you and yours were the objects of his deepest affection and his most earnest solicitude. You are the children of Abraham Lincoln. We are at best only his step-children: children by adoption, children by force of circumstances and necessity. To you it especially belongs to sound his praises, to preserve and perpetuate his memory, to multiply his statues, to hang his pictures high upon your walls, and commend his example, for to you he was a great and glorious friend and benefactor. Instead of supplanting you at this altar, we would exhort you to build high his monuments; let them be of the most costly material, of the most

cunning workmanship; let their forms be symmetrical, beauti
ful, and perfect let their bases be upon solid rocks, and
their summits lean against the unchanging blue, overhanging
sky and let them endure forever! But while in the abun
dance of your wealth, and in the fulness of your just and
patriotic devotion, you do all this, we entreat you to despise
not the humble offering we this day unveil to view: for while
Abraham Lincoln saved for you a country, he delivered us
from a bondage, according to Jefferson one hour of which was
worse than ages of the oppression your fathers rose in
rebellion to oppose.

Fellow citizens, ours is no new born zeal and devotion merely
a thing of this occasion. The name of Abraham Lincoln was
near and dear to our hearts in the darkest and most perilous
hours of the Republic. We were no more ashamed of him
when shrouded in clouds of darkness, of doubt, and defeat
than when we saw him crowned with victory, honor, and glory.
Our faith in him was often taxed and strained to the utter-
most, but it never failed. When he tarried long in the
mountain; when he strangely told us that we were the cause
of the war; when he still more strangely told us to leave the
land in which we were born; when he refused to employ our
arms in defence of the Union; when, after accepting our
services as colored soldiers, he refused to retaliate our murder
and torture as colored prisoners; when he told us he would
save the Union if he could with slavery; when he revoked the
Proclamation of Emancipation of General Frémont; when he
refused to remove the popular commander of the Army of the
Potomac in the days of its inaction and defeat, who was more
anxious in his efforts to protect slavery than to suppress rebel
lion when we saw all this, and more, we were at times grieved,
stunned and greatly bewildered; but our hearts believed while
they ached and bled. Nor was this, even at that time a blind
and unreasoning superstition. Despite the mist and haze

that surrounded him; despite the tumult, the hurry, and
confusion of the hour, we were able to take a comprehensive
view of Abraham Lincoln, and to make reasonable allowance
for the circumstances of his position. We saw him, measured
him, and estimated him; not by stray utterances to injudicious
and tedious delegations, who often tried his patience; not by
isolated facts torn from their connection; not by any partial
and imperfect glimpses, caught at inopportune moments: but
by a broad survey, in the light of the stern logic of great
events, and in view of that divinity which shapes our ends,
rough hew them how we will, we came to the conclusion that
the hour and the man of our redemption had somehow met
in the person of Abraham Lincoln. It mattered little to us
what language he might employ on special occasions; it
mattered little to us, when we fully knew him, whether he
was swift or slow in his movements; it was enough for us
that Abraham Lincoln was at the head of a great movement,
and was in living and earnest sympathy with that movement,
which, in the nature of things, must go on until slavery should
be uttterly and forever abolished in the United States.

When, therefore, it shall be asked what we have to do with
the memory of Abraham Lincoln, or what Abraham Lincoln
had to do with us, the answer is ready, full, and complete.
Though he loved Cæsar less than Rome, though the Union
was more to him than our freedom or our future, under
his wise and beneficent rule we saw ourselves gradually
lifted from the depths of slavery to the heights of liberty
and manhood; under his wise and beneficent rule, and by
measures approved and vigorously pressed by him, we saw
that the handwriting of ages, in the form of prejudice and
proscription, was rapidly fading away from the face of our
whole country; under his rule, and in due time, about as
soon after all as the country could tolerate the strange
spectacle, we saw our brave sons and brothers laying off the

..... of bondage, and being clothed all over in the blue
..... of the soldiers of the United States; under his
r..... two hundred thousand of our dark and dusky
..... responded to the call of Abraham Lincoln, and with
..... on their shoulders, and eagles on their buttons,
time ..... footsteps to liberty and union under the
..... under his rule we saw the independence
of the ..... republic of Hayti, the special object of slaveholding
..... aversion and horror, fully recognized, and her minister,
a colored gentleman, duly received here in the city of Washing,
..... rule we saw the infernal slave-trade which so
long ..... the nation abolished, and slavery abolished
in the ..... of Columbia; under his rule we saw for the
first ..... against the foreign slave-trade
and ..... treated like any other pirates or
murderers, ... assisted by the greatest captain of
..... the Confederate States,
less ..... must be slaves, and
slaves ..... and scattered to the four
winds ..... the fullness of time, we saw
Abra ..... the slaveholders three months'
grace ..... hateful slave system, pending
the ..... though special in its language,
we ..... effect, making slavery for
ever ..... United States. Though we waited
long ..... this and more.

..... of any white man friendly to the
..... forget the night which followed
the ..... January 1863, when the world was to
see ..... Abraham Lincoln would prove to be as good as his
..... that memorable night when in
a ..... watched at a public meeting,
w ..... not less anxious than myself for
..... which we have heard read to-day

Nor shall I ever forget the outburst of joy and thanksgiving that rent the air when the lightning brought to us the emancipation proclamation. In that happy hour we forgot all delay, and forgot all tardiness, forgot that the President had bribed the rebels to lay down their arms by a promise to withhold the bolt which would smite the slave system with destruction; and we were thenceforward willing to allow the President all the latitude of time, phraseology, and every honorable device that statesmanship might require for the achievement of a great and beneficent measure of liberty and progress.

Fellow-citizens, there is little necessity on this occasion to speak at length and critically of this great and good man, and of his high mission in the world. That ground has been fully occupied and completely covered both here and elsewhere. The whole field of fact and fancy has been gleaned and garnered. Any man can say things that are true of Abraham Lincoln, but no man can say anything that is new of Abraham Lincoln. His personal traits and public acts are better known to the American people than are those of any other man of his age. He was a mystery to no man who saw him and heard him. Though high in position, the humblest could approach him and feel at home in his presence. Though deep, he was transparent; though strong, he was gentle; though decided and pronounced in his convictions, he was tolerant towards those who differed from him, and patient under reproaches. Even those who only knew him through his public utterances obtained a tolerably clear idea of his character and his personality. The image of the man went out with his words, and those who read them, knew him.

I have said that President Lincoln was a white man and shared the prejudices common to his countrymen towards

the colored race. Looking back to his times and to the
condition of his country, we are compelled to admit that
this unfriendly feeling on his part may be safely set down
as one element of his wonderful success. organizing the
loyal American people for the tremendous conflict before
them, and bringing them safely through that conflict. His
great mission was to accomplish two things: first, to save
his country from dismemberment and ruin, and, to
free his country from the great crime of slavery. To do
one or the other, or both, he must have the earnest sympathy
and the powerful co-operation of his loyal fellow-countrymen.
Without this primary and essential condition to success his
efforts must have been vain and utterly fruitless. Had he
put the abolition of slavery before the salvation of the
Union, he would have inevitably driven from him a powerful
class of the American people and rendered resistance to
rebellion impossible. Viewed from the genuine abolition
ground, Mr. Lincoln seemed tardy, cold, dull, and indifferent;
but measuring him by the sentiment of his country, a
sentiment he was bound as a statesman to consult, he was
swift, zealous, radical, and determined.

Though Mr. Lincoln shared the prejudices of his white
fellow-countrymen against the negro, it is hardly necessary
to say that in his heart of hearts he loathed and hated
slavery.[1] The man who could say, "Fondly do we hope, fer-
vently do we pray, that this mighty scourge of war shall
soon pass away, yet if God wills it continue till all the
wealth piled by two hundred years of bondage shall have
been wasted, and each drop of blood drawn by the lash
shall have been paid for by one drawn by the sword, the

[1] "I am naturally anti-slavery. If slavery is not wrong, nothing is wrong. I cannot remember when I did not so think and feel."—*Mr. Lincoln to Mr. Hodges, of Kentucky, April 4, 1864.*

judgments of the Lord are true and righteous altogether," gives all needed proof of his feeling on the subject of slavery. He was willing, while the South was loyal, that it should have its pound of flesh, because he thought that it was so nominated in the bond; but farther than this no earthly power could make him go.

Fellow citizens, whatever else in this world may be partial, unjust, and uncertain, time, time! is impartial, just, and certain in its action. In the realm of mind, as well as in the realm of matter, it is a great worker, and often works wonders. The honest and comprehensive statesman, clearly discerning the needs of his country, and earnestly endeavoring to do his whole duty, though covered and blistered with reproaches, may safely leave his course to the silent judgment of time. Few great public men have ever been the victims of fiercer denunciation than Abraham Lincoln was during his administration. He was often wounded in the house of his friends. Reproaches came thick and fast upon him from within and from without, and from opposite quarters. He was assailed by Abolitionists; he was assailed by slaveholders; he was assailed by the men who were for peace at any price; he was assailed by those who were for a more vigorous prosecution of the war; he was assailed for not making the war an abolition war; and he was most bitterly assailed for making the war an abolition war.

But now behold the change; the judgment of the present hour is that taking him for all in all, measuring the tremendous magnitude of the work before him, considering the necessary means to ends, and surveying the end from the beginning, infinite wisdom has seldom sent any man into the world better fitted for his mission than Abraham Lincoln. His birth, his training, and his natural endowments, both mental and physical, were strongly in his favor. Born and reared among the lowly, a stranger to wealth and luxury, compelled to grapple single-handed with the flintiest hardships of life, from tender youth to sturdy manhood, he grew strong in the manly and heroic qualities demanded by the great mission to which he was called by the votes of his countrymen. The hard condition of his early life, which would have depressed and broken down weaker men, only gave greater life, vigor, and buoyancy to the heroic spirit of Abraham Lincoln. He was ready for any kind and any quality of work. What other young men dreaded in the shape of toil, he took hold of with the utmost cheerfulness.

> A spade, a rake, a hoe,
> A pick, a crowbar, a bill,
> A hook to reap, a scythe to mow,
> A flail, or what you will

All day long he could split heavy rails in the woods, and half the night long he would study his English Grammar by the uncertain flare and glare of the light made by a pine-knot. He was at home with his axe, with his maul, with glut and his wedges, and he was equally at home on water, with his oars and his poles, with his planks, and with his boat loads. And whether in his flat-boat on the Mississippi river or at the fireside of his frontier cabin, he was a man of work. A son of toil himself, he was linked in true sentiments with the sons of toil in every loyal part of the Republic. This very fact gave him tremendous power with the American people and materially contributed not only to his election to the Presidency, but in sustaining his administration of the Government.

From his inauguration as President of the United States, under his great office assumed under the most favorable conditions, position and strain the largest abilities. Not only was he confronted by a tremendous crisis. He was called upon not only to administer the Government, but to solve the problems upon be holds the fate of the Republic

A formidable rebellion rose in his path before him; the Union was already practically dissolved; his country was torn and rent asunder at the centre. Hostile armies were already organized against the Republic, armed with the munitions of war which the Republic had provided for its own defence. The tremendous question for him to decide was whether his country should survive the crisis and flourish, or be dismembered and perish. His predecessor in office had already decided the question in favor of national dismemberment, by denying to it the right of self defence and self-preservation—a right which belongs to the meanest insect.

Happily for the country, happily for you and for me, the judgment of James Buchanan, the patrician, was not the judgment of Abraham Lincoln, the plebeian. He brought his strong common sense, sharpened in the school of adversity, to bear upon the question. He did not hesitate, he did not doubt, he did not falter; but at once resolved that at whatever peril, at whatever cost, the union of the States should be preserved. A patriot himself, his faith was strong and unwavering in the patriotism of his countrymen. Timid men said before Mr. Lincoln's inauguration, that we had seen the last President of the United States. A voice in influential quarters said " Let the Union slide." Some said that a Union maintained by the sword was worthless. Others said a rebellion of 8,000,000 cannot be suppressed; but in the midst of all this tumult and timidity, and against all this, Abraham Lincoln was clear in his duty, and had an oath in heaven. He calmly and bravely heard the voice of doubt and fear all around him; but he had an oath in heaven, and there was not power enough on the earth to make this honest boatman, back-woodsman, and broad-handed splitter of rails evade or violate that sacred oath. He had not been schooled in the ethics of slavery; his plain life had favored his love of truth. He had not been taught that treason

... perjury were the proof of honor and honesty. His moral
... against his saying one thing when he meant
... to ... which Abraham Lincoln had in himself
... ... cope was surprising and grand, but it was also
... and well founded. He knew the American people
... that they knew themselves, and his truth was based
... the knowledge.

... was the fourteenth day of April 1865, of which
... tenth anniversary is now and will ever remain
... day in the armies of this Republic. It was on
... this day while fierce and sanguinary rebellion
... last scenes of its desolating powers; while its
... forces and scattered before the invincible
... Grant and Sherman ... a great nation, born
... ... by war was already beginning to raise to the skies
... joy in the ... was settled,
... ... by the ... crime of slavery —
... ... a great ... It was a new crime, a
... No anger of the rebellion was to be
... the satisfaction of a hell track
... But ... good ... it was
... to ... able ... to save you and
... ... liberated.

... Lincoln had ... great ... ds
... ... great change of
... but his easy
... ... to see the end of his great
... down but gradually
... with heavy grief, and treas-
... ... laid he, by the red
... assassin's ... died without warning.
... man who knew Abraham
... ... his fidelity to union
... ... will

Fellow-citizens, I end, as I began, with congratulations. We have done a good work for our race to-day. In doing honor to the memory of our friend and liberator, we have been doing highest honors to ourselves and those who come after us: we have been fastening ourselves to a name and fame imperishable and immortal; we have also been detaching ourselves from a blighting scandal. When now it shall be said that the colored man is soulless, that he has no appreciation of benefits or benefactors; when the foul reproach of ingratitude is hurled at us, and it is attempted to scourge us beyond the range of human brotherhood, we may calmly point to the monument we have this day erected to the memory of Abraham Lincoln.

APPENDIX.

After the procession arrived upon the grounds the stand was soon filled with guests. Immediately behind the speaker's stand were seated President Grant, Senator Ferry, the members of the Cabinet, and the Justices of the Supreme Court; Senators Morton, Boutwell, Spencer, Sherman, Bruce, and others of the Senate; Assistant Secretary of the Treasury Conant, Hons. S. S. Cox, N. P. Banks, and other members of the House; the Japanese Minister, Sergeant-at-Arms French, Dr. C. C. Cox, Hon. W. B. Snell, Dr. J. B. Blake, the distinguished gentlemen who were to take part in the exercises, and many other distinguished personages.

The marine band, stationed at the right of the stand, opened the exercises by playing "Hail Columbia."

Prof. John M. Langston, Chairman of the National Committee of Arrangements, presided.

Bishop John M. Brown, of the African M. E. church, offered a devout prayer, during the utterance of which a solemn and reverential silence was maintained throughout the vast throng.

Hon. J. Henri Burch, of Louisiana, read the proclamation of emancipation, which was received with as much enthusiasm as if it had just been issued, and at the conclusion the Marseillaise hymn was played.

Prof. Langston explained that Rev. Wm. G. Elliott, who was to present the monument, had been unable to attend, and he introduced in his stead Mr. James E. Yeatman, President of the Western Sanitary Commission.

Mr. Yeatman said:

The Rev. Wm. G. Elliott, of St. Louis, to whom had been assigned the presentation of the monument for the acceptance and approval of those who had contributed the funds for its erection, and to give a short historical account of the same, has been prevented from doing so, and it has only been within the last few hours that I received notice that he could not be present and that I was requested to take his place, which I am but poorly qualified to do. Asking your kind and considerate indulgence, I shall proceed, as the representative and president of the Western Sanitary Commission, to whom was entrusted the contributions of the freedmen, and the expenditure of the same for the erection of a freedman's memorial at the National Capital.

It is perhaps proper that I should tell you how it was that a sanitary commission came to be entrusted with this work. The Commission, composed of Rev. Wm. G. Elliott, George Partridge, Carlos S. Greeley, Dr. J. B. Johnson, and James E. Yeatman, well-known Union citizens of St. Louis, were appointed by General John C. Fremont, and afterwards ratified by Secretary Stanton. Their duties, principally, were to look after the sick, to fit up and furnish hospitals, provide competent nurses, &c. But as the war progressed, their duties were greatly enlarged. The care of the families and orphans of soldiers, Union refugees, the freedmen, in short, all the humanities grew as

... of the war ... came under their charge. For these various purposes large ... of money, clothing, &c., were contributed and sent to them, and ... ... and judiciously expended. And finally, after the war was closed; ... the lamented, honored, and loved Lincoln had been so foully assassi... ... in this city, five dollars were sent to us the contribution of Charlotte Scott, a poor slave-woman, who, on hearing of the assassination of President Lincoln, went, in great distress, to her mistress that had been, for she was then free, and said to her: "The colored people have lost their best friend on earth! Mr. Lincoln was our best friend, and I will give five dollars of my wages towards erecting a monument to his memory." This money, this five dollars, this grain of mustard seed, contributed by Charlotte Scott in gratitude to her deliverer, was sent to us by her former master, Mr. P. Rucker, through the hands of General T. C. H. Smith, then in command of the military post of St. Louis, having received it from Mr. Rucker, who was a Union refugee from Virginia, having sought safety for himself and family in Marietta, Ohio, taking along with him Charlotte Scott, and perhaps others belonging to him. It was this five dollars that was the foundation of this beautiful and appropriate memorial which we now see before us. General Smith addressed a letter to me, conveying it, which was as follows:

ST. LOUIS, *April* 26, 1864.

JAMES E. YEATMAN, Esq.:

MY DEAR SIR: A poor negro woman, of Marietta, Ohio, one of those made free by President Lincoln's proclamation, proposes that a monument to their dead friend be erected by the colored people of the United States. She has handed to a person in Marietta five dollars as her contribution for the purpose. Such a monument would have a history more grand and touching than any of which we have account. Would it not be well to take up this suggestion and make it known to the freedmen?

Yours truly,

T. C. H. SMITH.

In compliance with General Smith's suggestion, I published his letter, with a card, stating that any desiring to contribute to a fund for such a purpose that the Western Sanitary Commission would receive the same and see that it was judiciously appropriated as intended. In response to this communication, liberal contributions were received from colored soldiers, under the command of General J. W. Davidson, headquarters at Natchez, Miss., amounting in all to $... This was subsequently increased from other sources to $16,242.

From the liberal contributions made in the first instance, we are led to believe that a very much larger sum would have been subscribed. But, as our determination was to have a free-will offering without solicitation, we determined to rest with what was voluntarily contributed.

Harriet Hosmer, one of America's greatest sculptors, asked for permission ... a design, which she did. It was one of great beauty and merit, and ... ... it ever be executed, it would have been one of the grandest and most ... monument a works of art ever erected in this or any other country. ... this the design has doubtless been seen by some that are ... ... It was published in the London *Art Journal* and other journals ... ... and other countries. I trust yet that the gratitude of the ... people will prompt them to execute this grand design. I now proceed to ... the history of the Lincoln Monument as adopted and executed.

... members of the Western Sanitary Commission, Rev. Wm. G. ... for me in the autumn of 1865, when visiting the studio of ... Ball, saw the group subsequently adopted, and was so much ... that he spoke strongly in its praise after returning to St. Louis. ... to Mr. Ball that the work was conceived and executed under ... of the news of Mr. Lincoln's assassination. No order for ... ... received, but Mr. Ball felt sure that the time would ... ... demand for it, and, at any rate, he felt an inward ... ... His aim was to present one single idea, representing the great work for the accomplishment of which Abraham Lincoln lived and died, and all accessory ideas are carefully excluded. Mr. Ball also determined not to part with it, except under such circumstances as to insure its just appreciation, not merely as a work of art, but as a labor of love — a tribute to American patriotism.

For several years it has stood there in its place, greatly admired, but not finding the direction of its rightful destination. But, when the artist heard of the possible use to which it might be put, as the memorial of freedom by the emancipated slaves themselves, he at once said that he should hold it with that view until the Commission were prepared to take action, and that the price to be paid would be altogether a secondary consideration. When the description was given to the other members of the Western Sanitary Commission they sent for photographs, four of which, presenting the group at different points of view, were taken in Florence, and forwarded to them. They at once decided to accept the design, and an order was given for its immediate execution in bronze, in accordance with the suggestions made by Mr. Ball. The original group was in Italian marble, and differs in some respects from the bronze group now to be inaugurated. In the original, the kneeling slave is represented as perfectly passive, receiving the boon of freedom from the hand of the great liberator. But the artist justly changed this, to bring the presentation nearer to the historical fact, by making the emancipated slave an agent in his own deliverance. He is accordingly represented as exerting his own strength with strained muscles in breaking the chain which had bound him. A far greater degree of dignity and vigor, as well as of historical accuracy, is thus in part The original was also changed by introducing, instead of an ideal slave the figure of a living man the last slave in Missouri taken up under the fugitive-slave law, and who was, at one time, rescued from his captors, who had transcended their legal authority, under the orders of the provost-marshal of St. Louis. His name was Archer Alexander, and his condition of bondage continued until the emancipation act became the law of the land. A photographic picture was sent to Mr. Ball, who has given both the features and bearing of the negro. The ideal group is thus converted into the actual truth of history without losing anything of its artistic conception and effect. The monument, in bronze, now inaugurated, was cast at the Royal foundry in Munich. An exact copy of the original group as just described by Mr. Ball has been executed by him in pure white Italian marble for the Western Sanitary Commission, and will be permanently placed, as "Lincoln's Memorial," in some public building of St. Louis. Of the eminent sculptor, Thomas Ball, to whose genius and love of country the whole of this work is due, it is unnecessary to speak. His design was accepted, after due enquiry, as distinct seeking, solely on its merits. But it is a source of congratulation to all lovers of the American Union that this monument, in memory of the people's President and the freedmen's best friend, is from the hand of one who not only stands in the foremost rank of living artists, but who is himself proud to be called an American citizen.

The amount paid Mr. Ball for the bronze group was $17,000, every cent of which has been remitted to him. So you have a finished monument all paid for. The Government appropriated $3,000 for the foundation and pedestal upon which the bronze group stands, making the cost in all $20,000. I have thus given you a brief history of the Freedmen's Memorial Monument, and how and why the Western Sanitary Commission came to have anything to do with it. To them it has been a labor of love. In the execution of the work they have exercised their best judgment, done freely as it could be done with the limited means they had to deal with, and leaving the rest with those who will follow to say how was it, or how well it had been done. Whatever of honor, whatever of glory belongs to this work, should be given to Charlotte Scott, the poor slave woman. Her offering of gratitude and love, like that of the widow's mite, will be treasured in Heaven when the wealth of those rich in this world's goods shall have passed away, and been forgotten.

Professor Langston, when receiving the statue, said:

In behalf of our entire nation, in behalf especially of the donors of the fund with which this monument you and your associates of the "Western Sanitary Commission" have been charged, I tender to you, sir, and through you the Commission, our sincere thanks for the prompt and wise performance of the trust and duty committed to your care. The finished and appropriate work of art presented by you we accept and dedicate through the ages in memory and honor of him who is to be forever known in the records of the world's history as the emancipator of the enslaved of our country. We unveil it to the gaze, the admiration of mankind.

Fellow-citizens, according to the arrangement of the order of exercises of this occasion, it has fallen to my lot to unveil this statue which we dedicate to-day; but we have with us the President of the United States, and it strikes me that it is altogether fit and proper to now ask him to take part in the exercises so far as to unveil this monument.

President Grant advanced to the front of the stand. A moment passed in the deepest silence, but when the President pulled the cord and the flags fell away, and the bronze figures were exposed to view, the people burst into spontaneous applause and exclamations of admiration. To the noisy manifestations of admiration were added the booming of cannon and the strains of the band, which struck up "Hail to the Chief."

Professor Langston then announced that, by request, an original poem had been contributed by a colored lady of New York, Miss Cordelia Ray, and it would be read by Mr. William E. Mathews of Baltimore. Mr Mathews stepped forward, amid applause, and read as follows:

To-day, O martyred chief, beneath the sun
We would unveil thy form; to thee who won
The applause of nations, for thy soul sincere,
A living tribute we would offer here.
'Twas thine not worlds to conquer, but men's hearts;
To change to balm the sting of slavery's darts;
In lowly charity thy joy to find,
And open "gates of mercy on mankind."
And so they come, the freed, with grateful gift,
From whose sad path the shadows thou didst lift.

Eleven years have rolled their seasons round
Since its most tragic close thy life-work found.
Yet through the vista of the vanished days
We see thee still, responsive to our gaze,
As ever to thy country's solemn needs.
Not regal coronets, but princely deeds,
Were thy chief diadem; of richer worth
Thy modest virtues than the gems of earth.
Staunch, honest, fervent in the purest cause,
Truth was thy guide; her mandates were thy laws.

Rare heroism, spotless purity;
The soul of Spartan's stern simplicity;
Such moral strength that gleams like burnished gold
Amid the doubt of men of weaker mold
Were thine. Called in thy country's sorest hour,
When brother knew not brother, mad for power,
To guide the helm through bloody deeps of war,
While distant nations gazed in anxious awe,
[illegible] the [illegible] thou didst fulfil
[illegible] with [illegible] will

Born to a destiny the most sublime,
Thou wert, O, Lincoln! in the march of time.
God bade thee pause—and bid the oppressed go free
Most glorious boon giv'n to humanity.
While slavery ruled the land, what deeds were done!
What tragedies enacted 'neath the sun!
Her page is blurred with records of defeat
Of lives heroic lived in silence meet
For the world's praise of woe, despair, and tears
The speechless agony of weary years!

Thou utterest the word, and Freedom fair
Rang her sweet bells on the clear winter air;
She waved her magic wand, and lo! from far
A long procession came! with many a scar.
Their brows were wrinkled in the bitter strife
Full many had said their sad farewell to life,
But on they hasten'd free—their shackles gone
The aged, young 'en infancy was borne
To offer unto thee loud peans of praise
Their happy tribute after saddest days.

A race set free ! The deed brought joy and light;
It bade calm justice from her sacred height,
When faith, and hope, and courage slowly waned,
Unfurl the stars and stripes, at last unstained!
The nations rolled acclaim from sea to sea,
And Heaven's vaults rang with Freedom's harmony
The angels 'mid the amaranths must have hush'd
Their chanted cadence, as upward rush'd
The hymn sublime ; and as the echoes pealed
God's ceaseless benison the action sealed.

As now we dedicate this shaft to thee,
True champion! in all humility
And solemn earnestness, we would erect
A monument invisible, undecked,
Save by our allied purpose to be true
To Freedom's loftiest precepts, so that through
The fiercest contests we may walk secure,
Fixed on foundations that may still endure
When granite shall have crumbled to decay
And generations passed from earth away

Exalted patriot! illustrious chief!
Thy life's immortal work compels belief.
To-day in radiance thy virtues shine,
And how can we a fitting garland twine ?
Thy crown most glorious is a ransomed race
High on our country's scroll we fondly trace
In lines of fadeless light that softly blend;
Emancipator, hero, martyr, friend!
While Freedom may her holy sceptre claim,
The world shall echo with "Our Lincoln's" name

CPSIA information can be obtained
at www.ICGtesting.com
Printed in the USA
BVOW09*1534060317

477876BV00003B/5/P